# Red Ceiling

Bridget Keating

I0808416

HAGIOS PRESS

**Library and Archives Canada Cataloguing in Publication**

Keating, Bridget
Red ceiling / Bridget Keating.

(Strike fire new authors series)
Poems.
ISBN 978-1-926710-17-4

I. Title. II. Series: Strike fire new authors series

PS8621.E236R42 2012 C811'.6 C2012-901533-4

Edited by Paul Wilson.
Designed and typeset by Donald Ward.
Cover art: untitled, by Roberto Lopez Lopez.
Cover design by Tanya Wolk, Go Giraffe Go Inc.
Set in Minion Pro.
Printed and bound in Canada.

The publishers gratefully acknowledge the assistance of the Saskatchewan Arts Board, The Canada Council for the Arts, and the Cultural Industries Development Fund (Saskatchewan Department of Culture, Youth & Recreation) in the production of this book.

HAGIOS PRESS
Box 33024 Cathedral PO
Regina SK S4T 7X2
www.hagiospress.com

*For my Grandmother Keating*

*For Ciarán*

# Contents

## What to do with Rage

Follow the grid past the marsh
where thousands of geese
gather in fall.

Remember their shrill chorus,
your brindle dog running in shallow
water, the birds startled into flight.

How earth lifted, became sky.

Find the field where skeletons
of old washers, rusting cars,
farm equipment drift in swaying
brome.

Thick, arthritic trees,
knotted and bowed.

The place hawks scatter bones,
flesh and sinew falling from sky.

There you will find rocks,
seeped bodies, thick veins,
branching lichen.

Look for one with an old woman's face.

Listen to her song
rising from land's marrow,
its bones.

This is where you will start over.

## Birth Memory

After the first birth, you are told the body
does not remember pain, an amnesia
buried like ancient rivers beneath the prairie.

You remember an old man's story of drilling for oil,
the land split open, steel penetrating
layers of rock, strata of time, miles
beneath the earth's surface, and the fish
from streams below bursting from pipes,
their wiry, silhouetted bodies
flying in the sunlight, gills
flapping, and the gulls
circling.

Years later, when the weight of a swollen river
spills again, dark, clotted with reeds,
from between your legs, the memory of the body
shakes you, a violent splitting.

Birth pain wells and surfaces in cells and tissues,
its knowledge carried by breath, passed
in the marrow of bone. Your ancestors
calling your son into the light,
the curve of his pearled spine.

Your grandmother tells you
dying is harder than having babies,
the slow passage more painful,
the body less willing to let go.

When you die, you wonder
if you will feel your son's head
tear through you once again,
hear him gasping
for air.

## When I was a child

I swam in the sloped coulee
the thin-veined ravine,
haloed with light, inhaled seeds,
my body brome and bitterroot.

There, brittle grass, beaver dams,
heavy July flies, fetid dampness, I felt
a snake against my bare feet,
circling my legs.

I touched its moist, ribbed body.

Pulled beneath the soil, I shed
skin, my mouth filled with clay and silt,
seeds sprouted in the pit of my stomach,
thick vines and hooked tendrils
clotted my throat.

My eyes, white eggs,
hatched swallows,
pointed wings took flight,
plucked dragonflies and moths from the sky,
returned to nest, wove twine and stone in my skull.

When I came back, I saw the old Polish woman in black,
her face and hair hooded,
perched like a crow in her garden,
slicing an apple.

She saw my bloodied knees,
understood what I had learned —

how knotted roots wither, unhinge,
the sting of serrated grass against skin,
the heat of torn earth
wedged beneath small fingernails:
dirt, scaled skin, silence.

## Stigmata

When we were old enough to understand sin,
after eating the body and drinking the blood of Christ
we prayed for stigmata, the blessings of Holy Wounds,
our foreheads jeweled with ruby pricks from thorns.

We asked for electric bolts of pain to hit us,
spread throughout our bodies — that we might see
the mystical apparition of rope marks on wrists,
odour of sanctity reeking from pores.

We read Butler's *Lives of the Saints*
stories of impalement and torture —
the bloodier the better.

How we draped ourselves across the couch,
threw back our heads with the ecstasy
and passion of a soap opera star,
posing like St. Theresa.

We understood the importance of sensuality and volupté,
large breasts and cleavage necessary for the performance
and we prayed for those too,
scouring Titian's paintings for the best pair.

When we first bled, our uterine lining shedding,
our bleeding, we were told,
was not holy,
but a curse.

And we were no ecstatics.

## Vaginal Prayer

In the operating room, my doctor asks
permission to pray before the procedure,
a morning ritual before he starts his rounds
of cutting and cauterizing —
surgeries for sagging bladders, hysterectomies,
cervical biopsies.

*Do I mind?* he asks.

What am I to say?

No one so close to my crotch
has ever made the request.

My feet and ankles strapped high in stirrups,
surgical lights spotting my vagina,
he closes his eyes, extends his arms,
palms open, prays for God's guidance,
and the health of my cervix, a blue mask
muffling his words.

Near my head, an Arab anesthesiologist sits
on a metal stool, waits for the invocation
to end before he administers
the spinal.

I think about the roses blooming in my garden,
their delicate pink petals lush, labial,
that soon they will dry, wither,
the end of summer near.

**I remember seeing your face**
(*for R.*)

My lover is ancient,
rising from broken rock
and rooted seed, his face
scalded by sun, his skin
frost cracked, touched by fire blight.

At night, spirits seep into his bones.

They dance, shift shape,
crouch, live in this cavern,
tell stories in markings of fine lines
sculpted in soft clay.

Their glazed tongues brush against my skin,
talons trace curve of leg,
ribs, my breasts.

They speak the language of wind,
words serrated obsidian,
thin blades of flesh.

My small hands touch his skin,
trace deep puncture wounds.

He must heal in the open air,
inhale breath from night sky,
sing, his hooked beak
carrying this song,
the story of wind currents
guiding him.

## Disappearing

There are spirits in the valley,
beneath the water, bloated
faces press against the lake's surface,
peer up at the sky.

I saw them when I was a child,
leaning over the small fishing boat,
my arm reaching out to touch
them as we passed by.

I imagined how I might sink beneath the weight of water.

My white body
suspended in darkness,
strands of hair floating like seaweed,
a wreath of twisted algae on my head,
my face a halo of blue —
an angel submerged in the murky abyss
of Katepwa Lake.

§

Years ago, divers found a car with two men inside —
their bodies still frozen beneath the freshly thawed lake.

They disappeared sometime after Christmas, drove
off the side of a narrow backroad, the one that winds
the glacial hills of the Qu'Appelle Valley, a settler road
with a steep drop off. People looked for them all winter,
suspected the lake swallowed them whole.

In the spring, they sent the divers in.

My grade six teacher set up his tripod on the beach,
captured the scene with his new video recorder —
the tow truck reeling the red sedan from the mouth of the lake,
threading it out slowly, heaving it from its cold womb,
the stench of stagnant water leaking from sludge-stained windows,
the engine heavy with weeds.

When they finally took the bodies out,
the bones in their hands were shattered
from trying to break the windows.

## The story of the girl in the wind

Scald Crow Woman buries placenta,
sows blood beneath a willow,
sings blessings, hands kneading
earth, fibrous roots.

She tells you the story about the woman
who relinquished her daughter to the wind,
wrapped the child in frayed linen,
held above her head the small body,
wisps of slender bone draped with soft skin,
an offering to make the child immortal.

The wind gods, their mouths
tendrils of spliced tongue, plucked
the girl from her mother's arms.

They gathered petals, fine dust, and feathers for skin,
embers for eyes, scent of lilacs for lips,
fashioned a chain of winged seeds
around her neck so she could fly.

When her mother realized what she had sacrificed,
she begged the gods to return her daughter.
her wails carried on currents to the sky.

## How to find solace

If you want to find a body in winter,
watch the sky.

You will be led by a murder of crows.

Wait for spring when the blanket of snow
thaws slowly —

the peak of an elbow, ice scarred flesh.
Stone-filled sockets.

Spring reveals what the land does not claim.

Know that she has been lulled
by the songs of soil, the whispers of rocks.

That snow has kept her from the blade of wind.

### *Oskana-ka-asateki*

Waking, you think about the bison bones
locked beneath veins of asphalt
below the belly of these streets,
how rutted arteries rest on a thick vein
of bones, a city built on slaughter.

Potshards of hoof and horn,
skull and pelvis, spirits
restless in their unmarked ossuary.

They say pewtered bones of men and women
bind these stacks, woven hair and teeth,
whispers from swollen mouths, smallpox scarred,
hollowed eyes sealed, blistered
fingers clawing iron ribs.

Last summer, one block south,
a woman was killed, shot in the face,
three boys, a gun aimed
from the backseat of a car.

Behind a neighbour's house,
a boy was torched, thrown in a
dumpster. Still alive, he climbed
out, his body sugared with light
December snow.

In the blue light of the morning,
you are woken by howling
in the street.

## Waterfowl

*(for Kelly)*

Now your brown hands are gnarled branches,
wind's cold breath seeped in bone, veins
frozen rivers in your arms.

Years cutting metal on scaffolding
and wisps of steel and metal, thin shards
lodged in your eyes. Twelve stories up
and the electricity still on,
the lines nearly touching the ends of your hair.

You stood on that ledge
and spread your arms like the wings of a crane
and imagined you could fly,
the song of water calling you.

When you were a boy,
your stepfather told you
never to shoot waterfowl
above a body of water,
then he did it anyway —
made you swim in a fetid swamp
to retrieve birds, one's wing still
flapping, its head submerged.

You said each time you were about to sink,
that something lifted you up,
pushed your head above water
so that you could breathe,
that one gasp of air sustaining you,
the birds' necks cradled in your arms.

## Accident, December 1996

*(for my father)*

To think of your face now,
the night you returned to the party,
December, just before Christmas.

You had gathered presents
scattered on the highway,
the flash of metallic paper
shining in headlights,
the bodies being loaded
into the back of the van.

Along the curve,
bits of broken metal,
bent and twisted,
the car in the ditch,
peaks of whipped snow
blackened from dirt and oil.

Our bodies, you said,
carry scars, trappings
of what we experience,
what we see.

For years, I've wanted to trace
with my fingers
the web of silk threads
around your blue eyes,
to free the winged bodies
caught in deep etchings.

## Mary at the restaurant

I first saw her waiting outside the restaurant
near the frozen grid, just off the main highway.

Glazed eyes peering through frosted windows,
hair, fiery tendrils, tongues clinging to frozen glass,
her face the colour of polished bone,
chiseled ice.

The children restless and crying,
December bodies stuffed in snowsuits and toques
in the back seat of a rusting station wagon.

She kept away from people,
fled when someone got too close,
her gait skittish,
desperate.

Once she came in, back bent,
head down, jut-ribbed,
thin as a deer in winter,
a ring of fresh hickeys, red and purple,
on her long, slender neck.

Her husband fed on her like a tick.

He was a regular at the restaurant,
grease-coated air, whorls of thick smoke,
sat with the others drinking coffee,
ordered open-face hot turkey sandwiches and fries — extra gravy,
looked at my crotch when he gave me his order,
his legs spread wide, tongue darting from his mouth,
teeth cracked, stained brown.

Each night I wiped his smell from the orange vinyl seats,
swept thick nicotine and fingernails off the table.

Just before Christmas, her youngest son
sent a letter to the local newspaper
asking for a tree from Santa.

She hung a string of green lights in the window,
the outline of a crooked fir tree.

After they moved, the town burned
a pyre of rotting carpets, pissed-stained
mattresses, a green couch without cushions,
without legs, sheets from the windows.

When I think of her now, I see her running
out into the field east of town, running
to get away, her body lean and hungry,
a deer bounding through deep snow,
eyes burning against the winter sky,
her tracks already blown in.

**Tonali (Nahuatl: *Destiny, fate*)**

Saturday, and the market crowded,
tables of fat, ridged pastries stretched
like giant brown fingers on tables,
cinnamon skin of the women dusted with flour,
flies, petaled eyes burst from sugared skulls.

You hear men hiss, tongues
darting like snakes, and the birdman
dressed in white calling you, offers
the future plucked from the beak of a canary.

*Oracle bird*, the man explains, his eyes blinded
by sun.

You watch the little bird perform, picking
crisp pieces of paper, small fortunes,
from a wooden box, her wings
clipped, dancing in the palm of his hand.

Long ago, their yellow bodies birthed
from the bellies of Spanish ships, carried
in the throats of Conquistadors
before they spilled disease
and death.

After, the land swelled with feathers, grew
wings, foreign tongues seduced
the sky, licked desert
irrigated with
blood.

Now, the sages claim, canaries
predict nothing good, bring only
the promise of suffering.

## Garlic Woman

She worked in the garlic fields up north,
planted fleshy cloves in fall, harvested
clusters of roots in late spring.

Leaves and bulbils filled her pockets,
stalks, their white and purple blossoms
a cluster of stars, grew from her eyes.

She hung strands of garlic on her front door
to ward off evil.

When she slept at night,
flakes of thin, silver skin,
layers of parchment,
lined the sheets of her bed,
the pungent scent woven
into the threads
of her pillow case.

She braided bulbs of garlic,
plaiting stalk over stalk,
weaving the story of her life.

Her first husband, a hard rock miner,
killed by a bomb,
when he crossed the picket line.

Her son, years later,
in the pen for murder,
how he beat a man to death
for no reason.

She said each day
the soil gave her a place
to steep her shaking hands.

## Frogs

The night she left him, she drove alone
along a rain-slicked highway,
wind battering the car.

She pulled over when she heard
thick and weighty thumps against the metal,
saw in the light
white eyes glistening
like moist eggs.

Thousands of frogs, their will to survive,
migrating to burrow beneath
the clay and mud of lake beds,
a passage to their winter home.

In the darkness, their singing,
the drenched echo of song
gave her hope.

**To reconstruct a face**
*(for my father)*

The night you worked in the embalming room,
sacred place of blood and body,
your hands pieced a puzzle of fragmented bone,
a young woman's skull
like a shattered vase.

You removed flecks
of her crystal mask,
peeled the veil of skin from her face,
glued a hundred slender fractures,
*lamina papyracea* —
labyrinth of skull.

The night your hands sculpted her face,
did you think of her birth?

The crowning of soft shell,
her descent,
the unhinging of bone.

Did you think about your own daughter?
How once, she came to you,
her five year old arms carrying
jagged shells of porcelain,
her small doll's face shattered?

The tears when you said
there was nothing you could do.

## Bus to Aguascalientes

The man in the white cowboy hat is smiling,
his eyes closed, and his face
a carving of thick lines
like cracked, thirsting
soil.

His lean, brown arms tell stories
of fields and desert, stark,
swollen sky.

You watch him sleeping, the night
torched with fires, pyres on the highway
directing traffic, lighting his face.

He is a migrant worker, flesh
smelling of damp earth, hands
burned raw, transplanted to the north long ago,
his family scattered like seeds.

Each day, they wait on street corners,
fill the backs of trucks, work hunched
and faceless in fields spilling with vines
and berries.

When he returns home, his hands,
worn and dry with longing, will touch
his wife's skin, her breasts
as soft and full as ripened fruit.

His tongue a rain-soaked root
wetting her body, vines
spreading from the darkness
between her legs.

## Thanksgiving Day, two houses over

Every second word is *fuck*.

And he's screaming, the boy with the new blue Ford
coated with last night's grit, a box of empties in the back.

Then, a chorus of pounding and cutting:
the nail gun, the saw, its teeth chewing lean pieces of fir.

After, he throws everything, metal smashing against wood,
nails bouncing off concrete, rolling toward the end of the drive-way,
his father's voice calm, measured.

Earlier, the neighbours took their children inside,
shut the windows.

I sit on the deck, watch small birds gathering
seeds in the elm, the leaves yellow fists, curled,
fallen among rocks.

I won't see them again until spring,
maybe early summer, sharp
blasts from a compressor startling them into flight.

## I watch my grandmother

After the snow falls,
a cluster of icicles,
a clenched fist curled,
wasting with meltwater's
slow trickle.

The curve of a dead branch
blanketed with snow
is a bent spine,
thin and frail.

At night,
under the street lamp,
ice crystals cover stark tree limbs,
a tangle of coarse silver wires
like my grandmother's hair.

The last time I saw her,
she writhed side to side,
the flaps of a green gown exposing white thighs,
bones protruding, wrists and ankles
bound to a bed's cold, metal frame.

Her long fingers,
bones jutting like twisted amber,
thin, bruised skin.

I tell her I am her granddaughter,
and hold her hand to my cheek.

Once she told me
women in China gathered around her
in crowded summer markets.

Their fingers,
reaching for her hair,
touched her face.

They asked whether
silkworms had rooted in her scalp
spun delicate threads,
a silver silk tapestry
shimmering in the swollen sun.

## Moth

Once a moth burst
through the small opening
of my father's ear,
a furious, winged birth.

The labour frenzied,
its body flapping against his eardrum,
pressed in the darkness of the tight canal,
the moth pushing toward the light.

First, a feathery antennae slipping through the hole,
grey bulge of eyes and tongue,
its wings, dust,
tiny scales trailing in the light,
the soul born from the skull's black passage.

**Deer**

Once we were carried
in the ribs of does,
birthed from their lean bodies
in brome and breadroot.

Buffalo berry stems,
bony, gnarled fingers,
arthritic hands
held stories of old

now forgotten

lost here
in this place
where blackbirds fall like rain,
glint of eyes reflected in headlights on highways.

Beyond bloated stalks of wheat,
night's black canopy,
slaughtered deer scattered among
yellow canola.

Once soil nourished us,
healed our blistered mouths,
our bodies now clotted streams.

We conjured bees,
carried them in our hands,
their language vibrating
on our tongues.

§

In a field in the valley,
a swarm of bees attacked the owner of a vegetable farm.

He lay among the potatoes,
a piece of raw meat, swollen,
hundreds of stings gilded his lips,
sealing his throat.

You thought of him when you saw
the deer's arched ribs,
a skinned claw rising from frozen earth,
fresh snow, crows scavenging,
the smell of death clinging to crisp, winter air,
spent shell casings nearby.

## Communion

For weeks, my grandmother lies dying,
her body withering wild grass at the end of summer,
slack skin tight against her face like the young woman she once was,
a slow descent, the body
clinging to life.

After her death a wild-sky,
slate grey dog came to me,
broken toothed, jut-ribbed,
along the hoof-rutted path
beneath the old cedars.

Copper eyed, moose-muscled face,
skin scabbed, his scent —
a tangle of pine, swollen roots,
the dampness of leaves.

His breath thick with death,
feathers and blood of a small bird
tangled at his lips.

He drank water from the streams and rivers in my hands,
tributaries of memory, the place
where my ancestors live.

I offered his tongue the ridged canyons of my fingers,
his teeth scraped the curved cup of my palms,
his nose pressed against the warmth of my skin.

## Weaning Moon

I.

The best time to wean a foal
is during the dark of the moon,
after her swollen belly births,
a letting of light.

To avoid flight, separate
the mare under Pisces,
when blood is in the lower legs,
pooled in the ankles or feet.

After weaning, when the mother has dried,
a sucking foal will bring her "back in".

This is called witch's milk, the colour of old bone,
dried straw.

II.

Your first child never suckled,
fed from a plastic glove,
its milk-filled fingers
full like udders.

You held her once, her creased lips
soft as petals, rooting
at your breast.

After you left her, your milk flowed for weeks,
clouding bath water, dripping on the bathroom sink,
staining sweaters.

You stayed in the darkness of your apartment
the blinds down, faint moonlight
creeping through slats.

Even now you feel her, a phantom
sensation, her mouth at your breast.

**A Letter to my Daughter**

Before your birth,
I carve your eyes,
the creases in your hands,
the ridges of your fingertips.

Cut bone to sculpt you from my body.

I gather shale
splintered rock
layered silt
to create memory.

The land offers you stories,
stains you with gleyed soil.

You are born on the day of the Revolution.
A head crowned with lights.

Matted down
damp wrinkled skin.
Eyes black pearls
cultured in womb.

Birthed from this charnel house,
blood and bone of ancestors,
weight of history,
body blanketed with marrow,
tongue stitched with stories.

Malintzin's blood flows through your veins.

This woman of grass,

mythical Nahua mother,
claims you as her daughter.
Swaddles your body in woven cloth,
kisses your face with ruby lips.
whispers in your ear.

Tells tales of cities with streets of silver and floating gardens.
Of women who wear thick masks,
their teeth painted.

They dance with forked heron feathers in the *cuicalli*.
Feast on maize. Drink *pulque*.

She tells you of the children who sleep
beneath blankets filled with quills and gold powder,
their necks lined with jade beads.

They celebrate your arrival with gifts
of stones and clay.

It was then that Itzpapalotl,
the clawed butterfly,
came for you.

Cursed with talons
fashioned from sculpted metal,
she longed to hold you,
clutched you between her lips,
carried you away to Tamoanchan,
the burial grounds of your ancestors.

There, she left you in the furrow of a tree,
its blood nectar nourishing you
until you grew with such strength and knowledge
that from your web of silk

scaled wings became your arms
and antennae your eyes.

In Tamoanchan,
you saw the others —
they, too, were taken
and, from ground bones and spilled blood,
borne anew.

Chrysalids woven in gold thread,
their bodies emerging
in the early morning light.

By this time,
your skin had darkened,
and your hair,
long and unbound,
woven with acanthus leaves,
fell to your waist.

You stained your face with yellow and red
and set out to gather pebbles of agate and chalcedony,
drawn by the singing of the dead.

Do you remember this long passage?
It was marked with such silence
that, soon after,
words left us.

The stories no longer fell from tongues
but were carried, weightless and without meaning,
by the force of the wind,
and swallowed by the strength of the sky.

What was left was interred quietly beneath the ground.

## How Children Die

Some are claimed by forests,
dreaming beneath blanket of branches
in the boreal darkness, their gull eyes
lighting the search.

Like the girl who took a shortcut
on her way home and never returned,
lost in the embrace of evergreens.

Her twin sister watched
as she ran toward the path, the light
fading, a weaning moon
in the sky.

She imagines her sister now, a fossil
at the foot of a pine, petrified,
curled like a fetus.

Sometimes she feels her sister's
breath on her body, nails tracing
her skin, remembers when
water held them together.

## St. Anne's Cemetery, June 1981

The day lightning struck my father
digging a grave south of town
in the Catholic cemetery, I imagined
the swollen sky splitting, the beauty
of the light, and the heave from the blast
jolting him into the ground,
a caul of dirt and grass
draping his twisted neck,
the psalm song of pines
calling him awake.

Later, he lay in the hospital,
his neck split, sliced open,
column of bone fused,
the taste of metal on his tongue.

And the scar, a thick stalk, rooted
in spine.

Now, when he speaks of death,
he remembers the flared descent of the body,
how the skull brightens, blooms
with light, the kiss of current
tingling hands and hair
and legs.

## Relic

On the altar in the church, your small hands
trace the solid outline of stone,
touch its smooth surface licked
by a thousand tongues of water, sculpted
by old fingers, the slow lap
of glacial streams.

You are reassured by its firmness,
the thin black veins of its body, listen
to the singing bones encased in rock, imagine
bits of teeth and skull, a femur, white
as sun-bleached roots, and the smell of the dead —
clay and mineral and wet earth,
scent of last night's storm.

The marrow is a hive, combed,
waxen, jewelled with antennae and eyes,
a nest of bees, the brood
nursing on jelly.

Sometimes at mass you search
the mural of Christ, kneeling, his hands
extended toward a wounded sky, the canvas
pierced with two black holes
hollowed by bullets.

That was the time a young man
after strangling his mother
tried to shoot the priest, voices
sharp and heavy in his head.

Still, the punctures remain,
and you imagine what that darkness holds,
preserves in the slight space between brick and
canvas, how you might find a spider's carapace
dusted with mortar, wisps of feathers, seeds
blown from a field south of town, sprouts
of wheat unfurling like small hands
stretching toward light.

**When you leave**

I want to carry pieces of you —
strands of hair in my pocket,
the slightest eyelash,
husks of hangnails,
rub between my fingers filaments of dry skin,
scabs peeled from your arms,
stains from saliva on my shoulders.

Your eyes, stones
the colour of dried plums,
on my tongue.

**In Linares**

I breathe air weighted with death,
its sweetness on my tongue, sewer
rising through metal grates, meat
cooking at make-shift stands.

I stand above a Sheppard's body
its flattened skull,
teeth and hair, woven
with broken glass from bottles
on sweating pavement.

Here, they leave dead dogs to rot,
too many to pick up,
their stomachs bloated,
split open, grackles
drinking from pooled
sockets.

The eyes of the street are scarred, blinded
by a thick cicatrix, scoured with wind,
desert sand, like the old man
who waits on the corner for work
each morning, the back of the truck packed
with brown bodies.

Nearby, women as old as the trees
along the river, press tortillas, finger tips
stained with cilantro, palms
scented with lime.

## Horses

How the taloned wind gripped your neck
when you flew from the horse, its muscled force
heaving your broken-winged body
into barbed-wire.

Spikes sharp as starlight, twisted
fingers, knotted like fists
sliced skin, tethered strands of
your hair, silk threads
winding in sunlight.

You were five years old,
your crying a thin song
piercing the sky, the wound
on your leg a tangle of chewed
skin, muscle laid bare to sun.

Your horse reared
when she saw your father,
seeing his huge hands,
hands that carried heavy blows.

That was before you and your mother
left, fled across the country,
your hair as thick and black as the horse's mane.

The last time you saw your father,
you stood over his withered
and beaten body in a hospital bed.

You felt the lean grace of your neck,
the strength of your arms and core,
felt the beauty of your scars, the power
of your legs, how you awoke each day
and they carried you.

## Hunger

Tereus, the watcher, cut Procne's tongue
before she sprouted her feathered robe,
pointed wings, and became swallow.

Without words, she wove
the secret of his rape into a tapestry
with threads of red and blue.

I've met women,
tongues long taken,
clamped and cut,
the root pulled from the throat.

Mostly, it happens slowly over time,
piecemeal, the tongue sliced in small chunks,
carved against the grain.

After, a wasting, their mouths
as small as a bird's. In darkness,
their starved lips sucking
splintered light like marrow
from cracked bones.

They never grew wings.

A friend tells me it's the mouth
that men fear most, our tongues,
our voices, our teeth.

She says it happens to female dogs
forced to mate, the ones
who run or fight.

Sometimes they remove teeth,
tape mouths when they resist,
force a bitch over the knee,
three men holding her legs.

They use rape racks,
leather straps binding
shoulders and hips.

*It protects the male,* they say.
*He always wants it,*
*regardless if she's ready or not*

## Hunger II

Because she left,
he starved the horses.

Held them in stalls without water,
without light.

She left because
he starved her, her lips
bruised plums, heart
withering barley heads in drought.

Because she left
each night coyotes called
and the sleepless man dreamed,
wide-eyed, death shuddering across
fields of purple flax.

His neighbours said they smelled
the hunger, how it seeped
thick into truck cabs
when they drove past.

In fall, the man, broken
and drunk, taken by darkness,
was killed in the middle of the night,
asleep at the wheel, the roaring
air-brakes of a semi.

Years later, and the house sits
empty, just off the highway, faded white,
a red barn collapsing, phantom horses
running in long grass.

## Coyote Tracks

When I drive along the gravel road
west of the city, a doe,
blinded by a truck's headlights,
lay in the ditch, her neck twisted,
still alive, her eyes open.

I think about the coyotes
that will come through night.
It doesn't take long for scavengers
to catch the smell of a wounded animal.

In a few days, the doe's body
will be shreds of sinew, bone
gnawed, dragged,
traces of coyote tracks in dry soil,
crows already gathering.

I think about my friend, how three men
dropped her off along this road
on an August night,
made her walk back to the city.

Her blond hair
long and loose, large brown eyes
searching the night,
running toward the lights.

## Our Lady of Tundra Swans

She is from the north, the woman
with the scar on her back.

Fire seared her flesh,
traced wings
along her shoulders.

Her scorched skin
unfurled, bloomed
like fireweed,
feet and legs
beaded pink petals.

Now she travels far
from bloodroot and trillium,
her boreal womb, she skins
sinew from wind, hide from rock,
hands begging bowls, searching
for god, only to find herself.

What she carries with her are her birds,
aureole of ptarmigan and tundra swans,
their swollen spring bodies
longing to return to nesting grounds,
the frozen, white land
dancing with bright wings.

The birds rise, gripping her arms,
her flight graceful, sinuous,
the sun blinding, a silver,
sheltering sky.

## How to write poem for your grandmother who is dying

Gather her garnet ridged fingers in your hands. Trace
milk opal veins, narrow ribbons of river running
up and down her arms. Cut swatches
of her blue dress for a quilt. The quilt
will keep you warm at night.
Wrap it around your body.
Now breathe the scent
of her skin.

## Conjuring bats

When my son was three,
he knew the name for a medicine stick,
a sacred spirit-caller bound with buffalo skin,
eagle feathers, fur and bones of animals.

He told me the theory of Pangea,
that all life came from cyanobacteria.

He told me about the end of the world.

When he was four, he saw a man,
his arms like wings
holding the back of our Jeep,
keeping it from sliding
over the edge of an icy hill.

Now, he conjures bats,
lifts his arms to the sky,
whispers to them, invites
the winged creatures
to roost in our house.

At dusk, they arrive,
swooping from elm trees,
rattling the eaves troughs,
claws scratching the windows,
searching cracks in the siding
to get in.

He tells me they always return
to the place where their ancestors lived,
that, perhaps, they smell the bones
piled inside the walls of our home.

## Museo de las Momias de Guanajuato: a Guide

*. . . law required relatives to pay a tax to keep the bodies in the cemetery. If the relatives could not pay this tax, they would lose the right to the burial place, and the dead bodies were disinterred to make way for new arrivals. Later, they were put on display.*

– Museo de las Momias de Guanajuato

First, listen for the singing, bodies
propped behind glass tombs, coppered skin
stretched like vellum, haloed
with pale yellow light, mouths
open, a choir of the dead.

Remember what the poet said —
the eyes are the last to die.

Smell ripened scent of soil: tin, lead,
mercury, alkaline. Know the bodies are preserved
by the land, embalmed by the earth, hair and teeth
dusted with gold.

Imagine their tongues, how they tasted
salt-stained flesh, flicked curve of collar bone,
traced lips of lovers.

How the woman with the braided hair
felt the letting of milk, her nipples
hardening, the suckling mouths of babies.

Now, move closer. You will see your face,
transparent, reflected in glass.

§

When you arrive at the shelves,
you will find rows of babies, one fetus
removed post-mortem.

These are los angelitos,
baptised in white dresses,
filigree of lace stained pink from soil,
hands clasped in prayer.

Think about the time your mother
told you the cemetery flooded, the place
where your sister lay. You dreamt the small,
velvet casket buoyed, floated
into the town's lake. How it shone
in the sunlight.

And, the first time you saw the body of a child,
a young girl in a yellow dress, white polka dots,
her nails painted pink.

She was your classmate's sister.

§

When you leave, know that you carry
the dead on your skin, in your lungs,
their cells floating in the museum air.

That the clay masks you buy from the old woman
sitting in shadows beneath colonial pillars
are made of earth that preserved those bodies.

Now, they are in your home,
displayed on your kitchen counter,
the masks, traces of skin and bone,
the cat's feet scattering the dead
as they walk across the tiles.

## For Ignacia, Woman Buried Alive

*. . . in some cases, the dying were buried alive by accident. As a result, some of the mummies have horrific expressions attesting to their death in the tombs.*

– Museo de las Momias de Guanajuato

Ignacia, when you awoke in darkness,
eyes searching amnion of earth,
did fire opals
bring you light?

There, in your grave,
your arms seeking breath of desert,
memory of sky, you traced
the wings of butterflies
in grains of sand.

Roots of oak, gnarled fingers
twisted in hair, held you, sang
prayers of thirst and rain,
your mouth, cocooned
with copper, seeds of desert willow,
sucked rich silver veins,
the taste of cajete and honey
on your tongue.

Did you feel the streams and rivers
beneath your belly?

The water's song lulling you to sleep,
you dreamt of old women,
heads and bodies draped in flowered sheets,
eyes like pearl onions
peeled by the sun.

## Nipawi

*(for Dianne)*

Now you stand near the river, return to this waiting place,
away from broken streets, their flecked veins littered, shards of bone

shining like porcelain beneath blue lights. Your muscled legs
grow roots along the river's edge, skin thick and scaled

like the face of pines. You call out, speak the language of crows,
gather sticks and bones tongued by slow moving currents.

When night arrives, you dream of your first child and the child you were.
When he was born, his belly sliced open, a gutted fish, the surgeon's large

hands tearing into his small body. After, you held him against your breast,
your long hair braided with young branches, yellow pollen, needles

shedding silvery sheaths. You ran to the place near the water where
the women waited, their ghost hands healing his glistening body beneath

the pale light of a winter moon.

## My father

My father carries stories of death
thin and sharp as a blade
used for gutting.

In early morning, he gathers bodies
from winter snares, hooks
slippery, scaled flesh
from streams.

Sometimes he hears their bones singing,
traces thick scars woven in skin,
says the eyes are hollowed shells.

I remember women arriving at our home,
withered with grief, bringing gifts,
blankets and berries, sweetgrass braided
and bundled, their children's bodies
cold and smooth as river stone.

Now he carries seeds in his hands,
sage and wolf-willow, hips
from wild roses, scatters
them in the place
where he will die.

He points to the valley, how
water's carved its clay banks,
walks down to the river bed
where he will gather stones.

## Pigeons

The child with the twisted leg is learning
the paths of birds — crows, merlins, gulls,
small speckled ones for which he has no name.

Most days he sits in the ally, watching the sky,
his eyes black as a moonless night, tracing
patterns of flight on paper, a different colour
for each bird.

Crows are bright yellow, lines
sharp and deliberate.

For pigeons, he draws fat, gliding purple strokes.
He thinks they look proud, backs arched, breasts
thrust out.

Sometimes he finds fragments of white and blue
shells shattered like porcelain.

He keeps them safe in his pocket, secrets,
a nest of thread and feathers.

From his bedroom, the walls papered
with sketches of flight, invisible wings,
he calls pigeons roosting on eaves,
the chimneys.

When they land on his window sill, he places
his secrets in their beaks, messengers
who will scatter them among fields of canola
and flax, the yellow and purple flowers
swaying in the wind.

## The Root Cellar

When my grandmother was a child, she gathered rhubarb
in early summer, crabapples in late August,
chokecherries when berries hung like congealed blood
from branches.

In the kitchen, the air syrupy, she worked for days,
canning fruit, making jams and jellies,
rhubarb wine.

Recipes, battered scraps of yellowed paper,
hand-written notes in the margins, small details
smudged with grease, stained with juice,
flour wedged along the spine.

When she finished, she carried the coral jellies
and pulpy preserves to the root cellar, stacked
bottles of rhubarb wine on shelves.

All winter and into next summer, they sat in darkness,
her mother hoarding the preserves until thick blossoms
petaled, webbed white and green, apples, shriveled
faces of old women, rotted, and corks from sour wine
exploded in the middle of night, the splattered stains
dripping on cellar shelves.

## Red Ceiling

Night, the kitchen ceiling red, and its weight upon her shoulders,
the light dull when the generator slowed.

Those nights, she waited for his stories to end at the Legion —
the winter hunger in Holland, how bodies thin as death emerged
from bombed buildings. Children running behind tanks,
bare feet pierced with metal, begging for food.

Some stories were never spoken, but carried in muscle and sinew.

How she traced shrapnel beneath his skin, slivers of death,
ghosts brought home from across the sea. They slept beside her,
those ghosts screaming, their arms thrashing shadows in the dark bed.

## Magella

Magella birthed eleven babies,
never once left her house while they grew,
her belly blooming petaled hands,
budding eyes.

How each day from her kitchen
she traced the outlines of trees on glass panes,
recited the rosary, windows starched-
stained, smeared with finger prints.

The priest arrived every Saturday, communion
in the living room, slivers stitching her knees,
babies crying in the next room.

I imagine her red hair then, a halo,
fiery strands framing her face, a Pentecost
of pine needles on shoulders,
the wafer in her mouth.
I met Magella once,
her body as thin as a hungry hawk's,
bound in white sheets, withering
beneath florescent lights.

Then, her skull sunken beneath
the weight of air, her hair,
once the colour of flame,
grey as fine ash.

I always loved her name, said it
again and again, until it broke
from my tongue, a tide falling away.

## Story told in an antique store

They're all over the prairie, you know.
Back then, that's what happened. They
wrapped them up in old sheets, buried

them deep so the coyotes wouldn't get at them.
Sometimes the women did it. Held hands
over mouths until they stopped moving.

A blessing, really. We kept having them, and
we were all hungry. No one said anything.
And Val Marie so isolated my mother went crazy.

The prairie husked, wind peeling layers of land, howling
like the old crow woman who comes to collect the dead,
and the jaundiced sky dancing.

I remember the little, white box. My father
made it for the family down the way. That woman
was just skin and bones — her five children already sick.

The baby died soon after it was born. They took it
and buried it in the prairie. Like an animal,
I guess. I guess that's what we were — animals.

## Clothesline

Blue, in full view,
practical white cotton panties from Sears
like flags, a surrender.

At that age, you let it all hang out,
years of girdles and tummy control panty hose.

Where does she hang the naughty ones? The black lace?

The ones with feathers?

## In my garden

Buried beneath bulbous roots of roses,
gnarled bergamot fingers,
caul of clay-rich soil, sharp
bits of bone china, shards of plates,
flowers outlined in gold.

In my garden I poke and dig
a womb of rusting nails
and slinking polyps, pearl buttons,
iridescent fossils.

Last summer I planted a plum tree,
discovered the remains of a dress,
silk, thin and delicate as an old
woman's skin. I swept dirt from small bones,
chicken legs, fragments of wings.

Perhaps, they flew from the kitchen window,
a woman yelling,

*Cook your own damn chicken next time*

and the mound in the garden
growing like a tumor with each fight,
smothering primrose, pounding the peonies,
delphiniums bowing beneath the weight of buttons
and plates greased with gravy.

I'd like to think that woman cracked
a bottle of gin after, stripped
down to her slip, danced in the kitchen,
her bare feet marking up the green linoleum,
recently waxed and polished.

## Woman flies from Window, East Vancouver

The sidewalk smudged by the spit of old men,
ends of rolled cigarettes, and the woman's loose hair
splayed like prairie grass flattened from wind,
weight of heavy bodies, truck tires.

When she flew from the hotel window,
they said her belly shone, street lights
spotting her bare skin — how her body
arched, arms curved.

That after the glass broke, there
was silence, just silence, and her mouth
spilling soft tufts of curled down.

After they took her away, rain
cleaned what was left from the street.

The homeless went about their business
of bottle picking and dumpster diving,
steering their metal carts around
the bodies of dead pigeons.

## Sedna

It happens like that in stories —
women chained in towers, starving,
skin white as dried bone,
eyes eaten by darkness.

The hunger for flight,
to touch sky, birth
children with wings.

I like the ones about women
who shed skin like snakes,
talons springing from feet,
tongues barbed.

How they burrowed in men's throats,
escaped at night.

Others, like Sedna,
goddess of sea creatures,
became fish.

Her father pushed her overboard,
cut her fingers to release her grip.

How she birthed bear, walrus,
seal from severed fingers, body
sinking to ocean floor.

I love her monstrous beauty,
her legs fused, fat, forked fin
flashing in current, gills
carved in throat.

Even now we try to catch her,
lure her with shiny hooks,
drag her up, pound her head
with something blunt.

Then gut and scale her,
slice spine from meat.

## Lolita in a Shoebox

Clucking their tongues, the town's library ladies
wrapped the book in brown paper —
the kind used for sausage or steak,
and concealed it in a Simpson's box,
that held a pair of practical pumps, navy blue.

All winter, they exchanged the book
like agents trading secret codes in a musty basement,
the lighting poor, the hand-off silent, solemn,
the box hidden beneath long coats.

They spent nights sequestered
in steamy bathrooms, submerged
in water that drained cold, their white
bodies bloated and dimpled, toes
wrinkled like old crabapples
at the end of summer.

Townsfolk fretted about the ladies' strained looks,
deep frown lines and furrowed brows, dark circles
cresting beneath their eyes. They talked about
the dangers of reading, and how it could make
a good woman look haggard
and old before her time.

Folk didn't understand that behind locked
doors, beneath coats, wedged in tight girdles,
the eroticism of words, the pleasure of description
had taken hold of them.

How late at night, when they slipped into bed,
they dreamt of sensuous, young flesh,
the hands and mouths of boys,
not their husbands.

Once the inspection passed, the book
catalogued, and shelved, the names of borrowers
weren't recorded, the pages withered, stained by water,
small beads of sweat.

## Mating Ritual

In my mother's garden,
clotted soil spills vines,
weeds, thick stalks,
a season of neglect.

Silk moths as large as a man's hand
perch on bloated crabapples,
bruised, mottled hearts.

Cinnamon-speckled females
swollen with eggs
release their scent on the wind.

I watch the males' shuddering dance,
the incantation of flashing wings
spotted like purple eyes.

I remember the story my mother told —
how their tunic of grey silt
sweeps eye lids,
blinds.

Inside the house, she
lies awake, a rosary
wrapped around her fingers,
worry beads brought out against
darkness

## The Mourning Ritual of Crows

I am told crows carry the memory of their dead,
gather in the burning grounds,
flock to pyres where bodies burn.

That they practice rituals of mourning,
gather to wake the dead, their cries
an aria of grief.

Once, in early summer, I witnessed
their funerary procession, the frantic caws,
black silhouettes perched on sagging wires,
in my back alley, the body of a crow, its feet
curled toward sky, garbage strewn about.

They swooped at my head, covering
the corpse with grass, calling
for others to come, their vigil
lasting all day, and into
night.

## Red Star Woman

(*for Amber Redman*)

When she disappeared
the old women howled,
held eagle feathers to the sky,
rain falling on their withered faces.

They say feathers grew from her arms,
her body sprouted wings,
a bird wading through wind,
the night air cool beneath her arms.

That summer she danced
four days, four nights,
tangle of long black hair damp against her face,
wasps stinging the soles of her feet,
the valley's glacial spine
rising beneath her body.

That later her hollowed bones
scattered like seeds,
fragments rooted in clay,
the bloated hills of the Qu'Appelle Valley.

## After the fire

I walked past the charred house at the bottom of the valley, its frame
a black skeleton rising from land's white body. Early December, the air

crisp, and a woman searching scorched remains, her husband locked
in a fist of ice. When the river broke, its slow run heaving

silt and rock, the woman started digging, the spring thaw
birthing bones.

**Burns**
(*for Frank*)

Everyone in town said
the family pissed out the second-floor window,
the mother a drunk,
her three children from three men.

They remember the time the one with the long hair
brought a knife to school, the principal
dragging him into the office to get the strap,
the leather's thick tongue searing his flesh.

After, he soaked his raw hands in snow to cool the burn,
the welts rising on his palms.

No one ever talked about the time
he ran like a deer in the snow,
his sister's small body scalded,
a broken-winged bird
in his arms.

Her skin melted copper,
petaled flesh peeled
from boiling water.

How he carried her across the frozen lake,
chest heaving, pounding the ice,
blades of wind thrashing bare arms,
his black hair trailing in the January night.

**15 Block Rae St.**

From my bedroom window,
I watch the three sisters,
their nectar-fed bodies, addicted and desperate,
winged like fireflies, flickering in the humid July night,
moon-eyes full, shining under the street light.

The smallest one,
her cleft mouth sewn
when she was a child,
hair lustred, lank with sweat.

The oldest sister darts
in and out of the light.

The other, tall and wiry, waves her arms,
cigarette embers like small fireworks
in the dark.

On the street, in front of my house,
men circle, hunched over steering wheels,
trucks growling.

The sisters disappear with the beam of headlights,
the dull glow of the interior.

Along the sidewalk gutters, crickets chant,
a frenzy of moths batter themselves against the porch light.

## Field Sermon

You drive along the grid road
wedged between winter fields,

think about the time you stood
hunched on the back of a harvester,

sorting dirt and potatoes and rocks
pulled from valley fields. The loud

roar of that machine, masked faces,
dirt saturated bodies pressed together,

the fall sun drenching necks, sweat dripping
from foreheads. You caught your fingers

in the slight spaces of the conveyor belt.
Warning signs about the loss of hands

and arms posted in Spanish. How one day
the potato farmer stopped in the middle of the field,

gave you and the other workers a sermon about life
and death, the life cycle of wheat, how we return

back to the soil. Later, in January, your two friends
buried their brother, after his body lay in a coma

for nearly two years — that juncture where the body,
barely alive, survives, and death resists, the soul

parting long before the root of darkness takes hold.

## Eyes

I carry the fear of blindness,
its slow wasting a famine of light.

How it drowns lids, seeps
into dark coves, chokes roots.

Borges called this a gift —
*a hollow twilight, slow and precise.*

My mother's eyes are bright stones,
flecked jade. Before she was born,
they pearled in hollow sockets.

Now, they wither like her mother's eyes,
shadows unfurling like soft petals,
an endless night.

This spring, I want to plant
seeds that blossom with irises

pupils, sclera and retina,
eyes bursting from beds of rich soil.

How I'll pluck them, take
them to my mother, give her

new eyes, the stalks wrapped
with string.

## Kitchen Stories

Ask any kitchen floor,
and it won't tell you a thing.

They keep secrets, stories women tell
after supper, over kitchen sinks.

Births and hysterectomies, infidelity,
sex in a back alley in Italy or
the back seat of some car.

Once an aunt cornered me between a fridge
and hundreds of commemorative teaspoons,
snared and propped, hanging like slender
bodies against brown wallpaper,
rays of sunlight bouncing off the silver,
illuminating the walls like a disco ball,
Waylon Jennings on the radio.

Her advice on marriage:

*Men need it often or they go mad, just mad —*
*they get pent up like a pressure cooker*
*about to explode.*

And the stories about the grandmother I never knew,
how she made her husband sleep on a small cot,
no mattress, wire springs digging into his back,
a thin blanket. Later, she left, abandoned her children,
cooked in a fishing camp up north,
fled to Cuba for a new life.

She never sent any postcards.

One aunt told me about Paris,
her travels with girlfriends
when she was young.

She said she still imagines
herself there when she washes her floors,
on all fours, her knees and hands pressed
against the linoleum, and the Champs d'Élysées,
smell of cigarette smoke wafting from cafes,
high heels on cobblestone, the lights from the Grand Palais
guiding her in the night.

## Cihuateteo

Night, sweating womb of summer, and
pewtered streets birth
skull-faced women, bone-
lean shadow dancers
rising from caul of concrete
and dirt.

Heads crowned with rosehips
and burrs, feathers of grouse,
they cry, throat song of prairie,
haunting crossroads, the corner
of Robinson and $8^{th}$.

They are cihuateteo, spirits of women
searching for lost children. Their eyes
fevered opals, teeth carved with names,
faces tattooed on hands. They offer
swollen breasts, reach for barefoot children
who slip through eagle claws.

Their grief is sharp and jagged, shattered glass,
piercing night sky,
the air bloated and heavy.

Their wails wake chained dogs in fenced yards,
the barking a psalm of mourning.

**Harvest**

Each year men died,
drowning in silos of grain,
gold seeds lining mouths and lungs.

Some flew off platforms of elevators,
swooping like swallows, or pinned
by bulls against pens, pressure
bursting hearts, blood
pooling in eyes.

Sometimes it was slower —

Metal teeth chewing arms and legs,
chemicals coating the soft pink of throats,
their root-bound tongues withering, growing
so porous that currents of wind
swept them away.

How they sailed like kites
high above heads.

Others were scarred by sun, bodies
baked on tractors, purple blotches of skin
spreading each summer, the forehead,
the hands, the tips of noses.

This is the how the land bartered, after
generations of taking.

## How to make peace with yourself

Take the next bus, Broad Street North,
to the edge of the city where the fields
begin their yawn.

Before you sit down,
wipe chicken grease from blue,
cracked vinyl seats.

Now listen.

A woman, her face like a crow,
carries her children's teeth,
a cluster of pearls, in her pocket.

The man at the back,
body rotting, pants stained with urine,
sings his sorrow-song sharp as a sparrow's.

The young boy's silence,
staring out the window.

When the bus stops,
remember the times you were alone.

How you walked across a field as a child,
dreaming your fingers into feathers, the fall
wind whipping your pale shoulders, summer-fallow
stabbing your shins.

Your fingers become feathers,
your pale shoulders sprout wings.

Now fly.

**Sparrows**

My son says
no one ever notices sparrows.

*They are not pretty like other birds,*
*and they annoy people.*

Through the kitchen window
we watch them,
thin winter bodies
birthed from branches of elm trees.

He tells me
they carry the souls of the dead
on their wings, and clutch
the souls of newborns in their stubbed beaks.

My son, his quiet hunger,
body thirsting for attention,
understands this journey.

I carried him once,
a stone in my fertile belly
grew flesh and bone.

His arms became wings,
took flight.

He feels the sparrows' breath when they sing,
quiet songs gripped in earth's gut
rising from silt and rock beneath his feet.

## Montserrat Monastery

I.

We hike trails named for saints,
paths tracked by hermits, their caves
clefts molded in slate and quartz,
hollowed wombs tongued by wind and rain,
petrified flames, death's head
rising from land.

Stone fingers offer communion,
bones of slaughtered monks, spilled
blood, tenor of talons and wings,
solitude of sky.

II.

At the altar of the Black Virgin,
women offer their eyes, blindness
hung on hooks, pierced
hearts strung with pink ribbon,
breasts and kidneys,
roses bound with black feathers.

Here, they bring grief, beads
spilling from hands, shards of sorrow,
prayers for the sick and suffering,
frayed silk dresses stirring in fine light.

III.

At night, candles line a cobblestone alley,
thousands of flames, and a woman,
feathers sprouting from spine.

She holds death in her fists, its hunger
threaded and knotted in ribs, a weaving
of shell and rock, husks of stag beetles
peeling from lips.

How she broods, her eyes black gutters,
scaled skin slipping from bone and sinew,
wind chanting psalms.

IV.

A dog thin as air, dark
as night sky, paces,
searching for food, claws
scraping stone.

Ghost-like, sinewy,
he disappears in dark folds of rock,
a woman as old as sky, eyes
thick, sun-scarred, face
marked by wind's teeth.

Naked, she sings, her voice
rising from roots, trees suckling
breasts, ossuary of birds in belly.

She dreams bodies of dust,
fragments of honeycombed marrow,
remembers the fires, dancing
shadows in deep caverns.

V.

The monks, their black robes sweeping
marble, gather in the square.

On the last Thursday of each month,
they unhook eyes, remove hearts
and breasts from the altar.

Take down the silk dresses,
yellowing lace.

Black feathers dance on tile,
scent of rotting flowers,
the panicked flight of doves.

# Acknowledgements

Several of these poems have appeared in *Spring* and *Wording the World*. The italicized lines in "Eyes" are taken from Jorge Borges's poem, "The Gift of Darkness," which appears in *Poems of the Night*. In "Museo de las Momias de Guanajuato: a Guide," there is a reference to Edmond Jabès's "Show," found in *The Selected Poems of Edmond Jabès*.

I would like to thank Paul Wilson for his generosity, kindness, and encouragement; Olive Senior, for her guidance and mentorship, especially in the early development of this work; Randy Lundy, for his love and support; my son, who constantly inspires me; my family, friends, and my dogs.

Bridget Keating lives with her son, two dogs, and two cats in Regina. Her work has appeared in *Spring* and *Wording the World*, an Australian anthology of emerging and established poets. She has an MA from the University of Regina and has worked as a sessional lecturer at the University of Regina, Luther College, and First Nations University of Canada. She is currently working on her PhD, which explores representations of Mayan women in the Zapatista resistance movement. *Red Ceiling* is her first book.